SISTER MARY FAITH

YOU ARE MY SON

You Are My Son

iUniverse books may be ordered through booksellers or by contacting:

iUniverse
1663 Liberty Drive
Bloomington, IN 47403
www.iuniverse.com
844-349-9409

Because of the dynamic nature of the Internet, any web addresses or links contained in this book may have changed since publication and may no longer be valid. The views expressed in this work are solely those of the author and do not necessarily reflect the views of the publisher, and the publisher hereby disclaims any responsibility for them.

Any people depicted in stock imagery provided by Getty Images are models, and such images are being used for illustrative purposes only.
Certain stock imagery © Getty Images.

ISBN: 978-1-6632-0572-8 (sc)
ISBN: 978-1-6632-0574-2 (hc)
ISBN: 978-1-6632-0573-5 (e)

Library of Congress Control Number: 2020913393

Print information available on the last page.

iUniverse rev. date: 12/02/2020

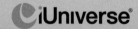

You Are My Son

You are my son. You started out as my baby.

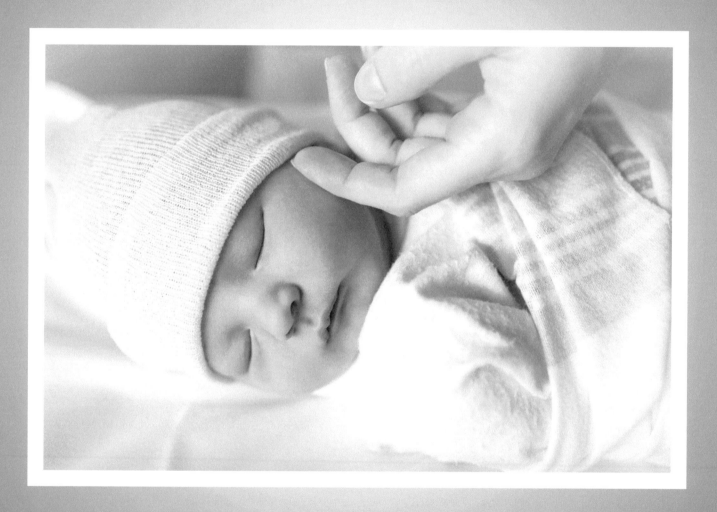

Though you haven't been born yet, I know you are going to have a wonderful life. Your dad and I have been talking about you. We promise to introduce you to your new life.

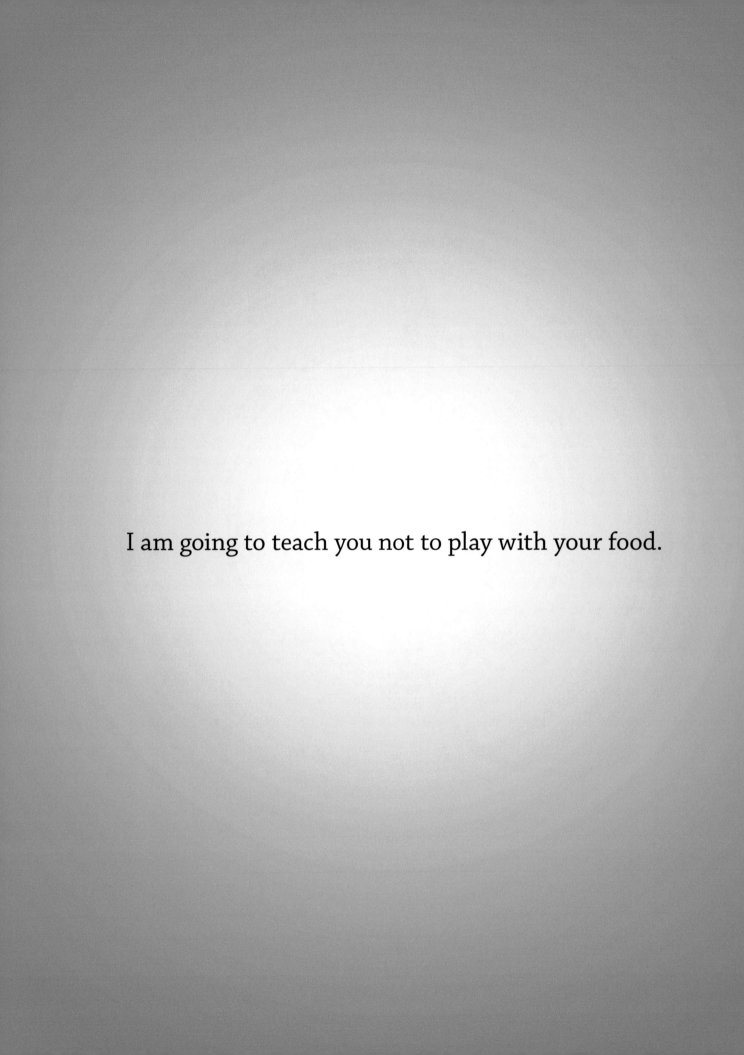

I am going to teach you not to play with your food.

We won't mean to startle you with the flash of light from the camera on your first birthday.

We will share the joys of the seasons. You will learn about football games, Halloween and haunted houses, Thanksgiving, Santa Claus, the Easter bunny, flying kites, and fireflies.

Your dad will teach you about high finance. He will start with the tooth fairy. He will teach you about contracts when you become the Little League's star pitcher.

I look forward to being your pack mom.
I am going to be so proud of you when
you are the Cub Scouts pack leader.

Your dad and I will be there when you receive your Eagle Scout award.

Then, it will be time for college. We promise
to love you, even if you don't graduate Summa
Cum Laude. I will still beam with pride
when I see you in your cap and gown.

I asked your dad if you could be president of the United States. He said you should probably be president of the Rotary Club first.

He's right.

Your dad and I have taught you all about the world
and how to make friends and influence others.

We have been with you each step of the
way. You are my pride and joy. Someday,
you will realize you are a man.

Grasp it, son.

Until now, I have been right here
beside you each step of the way.

I have stood just outside the limelight. I
want you to hold a graduate degree from my
school of life. If I have been the best teacher,
you won't think of me on graduation day.

I see a new woman in your future. I will
step back so you two may walk down
the aisle of love and life together.

You have left the nest. Fly high, my son. Sometimes,
bring my grandchildren to see me so I can tell them
what their old man was like when he was young.

It's a wonderful life. Enjoy it. Your whole life is laid out before me. Now, it is time for me to give birth to you. You are my son. Welcome to our world.

Printed in the United States
By Bookmasters